# Peanut, Peanut, Crack Your Shell

written & illustrated

by

Alexander Rega

*for*

*Amy & Anthony*

Peanut, peanut crack your shell.

How else is anyone to tell,

If you're a boy or you're a girl?

Come out, come out in to the world.

Peanut, peanut, come out to play.

I cannot wait to see your face;

To gaze in to your eyes so bright,

To smile at you, day and night.

Peanut, peanut, don't delay.

Rise and feel the light of day.

I'll squeeze you tight and hold you close.

I'll cherish and adore you most.

Peanut, peanut, no more sleep.
Arise and make a peanut peep.
Sing a melody for my ears,
A pleasant tune for all to hear.

Peanut, peanut, shed your husk.
Crinkle your nose and pucker up.
I have a peanut kiss for you.
You are my peanut wish come true.

Peanut, peanut, you are loved,
From seas, so deep, to stars above.
And, peanut, when your hard shell cracks,
I'll love you to the moon and back!

CPSIA information can be obtained
at www.ICGtesting.com
Printed in the USA
LVHW071031180219
607862LV00023B/309/P